BRENDON WATERS

Bait to Plate

How to Navigate, Attract & Shape Shift to Success In The Modern Music Industry

First published by House of Nuwara 2025

Copyright © 2025 by Brendon Waters

All rights reserved. No part of this publication may be reproduced, stored or transmitted in any form or by any means, electronic, mechanical, photocopying, recording, scanning, or otherwise without written permission from the publisher. It is illegal to copy this book, post it to a website, or distribute it by any other means without permission.

Brendon Waters asserts the moral right to be identified as the author of this work.

Brendon Waters has no responsibility for the persistence or accuracy of URLs for external or third-party Internet Websites referred to in this publication and does not guarantee that any content on such Websites is, or will remain, accurate or appropriate.

Designations used by companies to distinguish their products are often claimed as trademarks. All brand names and product names used in this book and on its cover are trade names, service marks, trademarks and registered trademarks of their respective owners. The publishers and the book are not associated with any product or vendor mentioned in this book. None of the companies referenced within the book have endorsed the book.

Cover design: Brendon Waters

Interior formatting by Brendon Waters

For permissions, press, or speaking inquiries:

www.houseofnuwara.com

House of Nuwara

Library of Congress Control Number: 2025920529

First edition

ISBN (paperback): 979-8-9994291-1-7
ISBN (hardcover): 979-8-9994291-2-4

This book was professionally typeset on Reedsy.
Find out more at reedsy.com

I dedicate this book to my parents for instilling music, faith, passion, and drive in me. To every manager, attorney, team member, and partner who believed, guided, or took a chance on me— thank you. To Sony Music Publishing and SESAC, I'm grateful for our lasting relationship. To every team member—thank you. Every deal, lesson, and even setback helped shape my path, sharpen my purpose, and prepare me to share, uplift, and thrive in this ever—evolving industry. Every step led me to purpose.

"I learned the hard way—by doing the wrong things first. But each misstep gave me something real. Now I share the game, not just to teach—but to heal, build, and guide with purpose."

- Brendon A. Waters

Contents

Foreword	iii
Preface	v
Acknowledgments	viii
Brief Biography of Brendon Allyn Waters	ix
Prologue	1
Introduction	3
1 The Roots of Your Creative Foundation	7
2 Discover Your Value	10
3 Studio Essentials, Workflow & Tools	13
4 Building Skills from Scratch	17
5 Learning the Business & Protecting Your Music	20
6 Networking With Intention	27
7 Understand The Assignment: Sync, Licensing & Placements	30
8 Leverage is The Long Term Play	34
9 Shapeshifting Into Ownership	37
10 Legacy, Longevity & Feeding the Future	44
11 Conclusion	50
Epilogue	51
Glossary of Music Industry Terms	53
Sources & Resources	57
Bonus Reflections & Mantras I	59
Bonus Reflections & Mantras II	60
Bonus Reflections & Mantras III	61
Bonus Reflections & Mantras IV	62
Bonus Reflections & Mantras V	63
Bonus Reflections & Mantras VI	64

Bonus Reflections & Mantras VII

Foreword

When Genesis[1] first entered my classroom at Clark Atlanta University, he was a quiet storm—curious, thoughtful, and deeply creative. He wasn't loud or boastful, but there was something about the way he engaged with ideas, how he questioned the world around him, and how he expressed his thoughts that made it clear: this young man was going somewhere.

Over time, I watched him evolve from a student with potential into an artist with purpose. He was always chasing meaning—whether in a sentence, a beat, or a vision. Even then, it was clear that his path wouldn't be traditional. Genesis wasn't just learning material for a grade; he was gathering tools, insights, and inspiration for a bigger assignment—one that would take him around the world and into rooms where stories are shaped and culture is made.

From Bait to Plate is more than a memoir—it's a map. It's the journey of a young Black man who refused to be defined by limitation, who let faith, hunger, and hard work carve his way from obscurity to influence. In this book, Genesis lays it all out: the struggles, the wins, the lessons learned behind the scenes, and the moments that nearly broke him but ultimately built him.

As a professor, few things bring greater joy than witnessing your students live out their purpose. And Genesis has done just that—writing his own lyrics, producing his own beats, and now, sharing his own truth in these pages.

This is not just his story—it's a testimony, a tool, and a torch for anyone daring to dream outside the box.

Enjoy the journey.

Dr. Carolyn Hall
Former Professor, Clark Atlanta University

---

[1] "Genesis" is the author's childhood nickname, used here by his college, Dr Carolyn Hall.

Educator, Author, Empowerment Coach

Preface

Feeding the Future: From Mama's Basement to Global Charts

I didn't start this journey in a mansion or with a golden spoon. I started in my mother's basement, trying to figure out how to turn a gift into something I could live on. Back then, success meant pressing up CDs and hustling them hand-to-hand, selling mixtapes out the trunk or at school, performing anywhere they'd hand me a mic. This was before social media became king, when your name traveled through flyers, open mics, word of mouth —somebody vouching for you in a conversation that you weren't even in.

I came up in a special era. The tail end of the analog hustle and the beginning of the digital age. I was a student of it all—studying the credits inside CD booklets, reading who produced the tracks, who wrote the lyrics, who the A&R was, who got thanked. I studied the bars. I studied the visuals. I paid homage. Michael, Prince, Bruce, Jay. And even the ones who moved different, like Chamillionaire, who showed us what it looked like to innovate before the rest caught on.

I grew up in Boston, Massachusetts—underground shows, battles, small stages, real grind. But I always had a bigger vision. I hit the road. Performed in New York City, the Apollos'. Auditioned and sign contracts for America's Got Talent. Got looks from TLC. Took that leap to Atlanta where I studied and lived in the middle of the music scene. The dorm room was my label office. The studio was wherever I could plug in a mic. I built relationships with engineers, interns, DJs, promoters, door girls, attorneys, and execs. I learned the industry inside and out—person to person.

Then came LA. Then came the films. The sync placements. The sessions that turned into Billboard hits. I wrote for major artists and sat in rooms with major companies—Atlantic, Sony, Warner, Disney, Fox. Worked on scores. Landed songs with legends. Built catalogs and creative businesses that feed my family now. I've had credits beside Wyclef, Tinashe, Drake, Lil Wayne, H.E.R., and alongside artists from around the globe—Avicii, Dan Balan, DJ Koze, and many more. This path has taken me across continents and cultures, building bridges through music and business alike.

But through all of it—what I learned is this: Your gift is the bait.
    The opportunity is the cast.

The value is what you reel in.

And the plate is what you build from it—what feeds you, your family, and your legacy.

That's what Bait to Plate is about. This is more than a book. It's a blueprint. It's a lived experience from someone who's shaped records, run deals, and shaped a business through the creative spirit. This is for the independent ones. The hungry ones. The visionaries. The quiet geniuses building catalogs in their bedrooms. The ones who know they've got something real, but just need to know how to move.

I'm here to show you how to move.

This book wasn't written—it was lived.
    Every word, insight, and process comes from real life. From the soundproof walls of my mother's basement to first-class flights next to aerospace execs. From jam-packed poetry nights to Grammy-level sessions in the Hills. From sync deals with Disney to countless "almosts" that still taught me something. This isn't theory—this is testimony.
    Bait to Plate was born as an audiobook, created in real-time, in free-

form—but molded from discipline, instinct, and over a decade of experience across every corner of today's music industry. I've been the producer, the songwriter, the one mixing vocals at 6 AM, the one negotiating sync fees, the one registering records, hiring musicologists to analyze and assess my proper shares, or the one getting left out of the split sheet or credits.

What you're holding now is the written form of everything I wish someone had told me. Every lesson, every mistake, every win—structured so you can read it, re-read it, and apply it. This is for the independent artist, the emerging exec, the producer in their first home studio. It's a navigation guide, a blueprint, and a mirror. Before you shape the industry, you've got to shape yourself. This book is your guide through every part of that process—from recognizing the bait, to casting it strategically, to building the systems that turn creativity into legacy. Every story, every section is a blueprint rooted in real experience. This isn't a theory. It's a process I lived.

Let's begin.

Acknowledgments

To the ones who saw me and my highest potential—
   my family, my day ones, my people.
   For the quiet supporters, the loud believers,
   and the ones who stood by me before the music had a name.
   You helped shaped the man behind the music.
   This book is for the believers, the builders,
   and every creative who is willing to find the way.
   To Our Father who art in heaven. Thank you for the light, the wisdom, and your guidance.

   Brendon Allyn Waters

Brief Biography of Brendon Allyn Waters

Brendon Waters, professionally known as, Marley Waters, is a genre-defying music producer, artist, and author whose career epitomizes the modern blueprint for independent success in the entertainment industry. From co-producing the Billboard #1, RIAA platinum-certified hit "2 On" by Tinashe to penning his debut book Bait to Plate: How to Navigate, Attract, and Shape-shift to Success in the Modern Music Industry, Waters has built a legacy fueled by strategy, self-belief, and unwavering innovation.

Born in Boston and forged in the hustle of Atlanta's music scene, Waters left college with just one year remaining—not out of defeat, but out of conviction. With a vision bigger than a classroom and a work ethic sharpened by real-life challenges, he transformed personal adversity into creative power. From a modest home studio in Los Angeles, he steadily carved a path to major success—earning a SESAC Pop Award, chart-topping credits, and licensing placements on cultural mainstays like Starz's Power, Showtime's The Chi, and Netflix's End of the Road.

What separates Waters is not just his hit records—but the way he thinks. His work is deeply intentional, strategically built, and culturally rooted. Now based in Johannesburg, South Africa, he draws from local influence to expand his sonic universe, blending African rhythms with global pop sensibility, and reshaping what it means to be an international artist in the digital age.

In 2025, Waters added "author" to his resume, publishing *Bait to Plate*—a practical, motivational, and experiential guide for creatives navigating the modern music business. More than a book, it is an industry toolkit powered by 15+ years of firsthand wins, losses, legal lessons, and breakthroughs. His mission? To break cycles of gatekeeping, democratize knowledge, and empower the next generation of artists and entrepreneurs to create from a place of clarity, ownership, and purpose.

Whether he's building catalogs, licensing soundtracks, speaking to creators, or investing in the next frontier of Web3 music platforms, Marley Waters is a creative force who operates beyond trends. He's not chasing virality—he's architecting longevity.

Prologue

Bait to Plate: How to Navigate, Attract, and Shape shift to Success in the Modern Music Industry wasn't written just to be read—it was written to be used. A tool. A voice of motivation. A mirror to your own potential.

This book is for the dreamers, the doers, and the ones trying to figure it out without a map. It's written from a place of experience—real trenches, real studios, real contracts, real breakthroughs. I've walked the path from the early days of just discovering my gift to standing in the rooms where deals are signed and checks get cut. I've made it work—survived and thrived—for over 15 years off the strength of my music, my mind, and my movement.

I wrote this because I want you to know:

You can do what you really want to do. You can create what you truly want to create.

But you'll need precision. Strategy. A deeper understanding. That's where this book comes in.

You'll get everything from basic industry knowledge to intermediate frameworks to more advanced ideas and approaches that will elevate your hustle. Much of what I share here is what was never shared with me. A lot of it was locked behind gatekeeping and closed doors—because unfortunately, that was part of the culture. But we're shifting that. I believe in passing the game forward.

So take notes. Highlight the gems. Treat this like a workshop, because there are calls to action throughout. But understand this: no matter how powerful these pages are, **you have to do the work.**

This is more than a book. It's a movement. A foundation.

A guide with real tools and real stories. I've included moments of self-reflection, personal lessons, and perspectives that helped me stay disciplined and focused—even when everything around me said quit.

You might find your blueprint here. You might just find your breakthrough.

And when you do—I hope you take the torch, run with it, and light up the path for someone else too.

Introduction

Before there was a book, there was an irresistible pull. A calling. Not for recognition. Not even for the reassuring nod of validation. There was simply an undeniable urge—an intentional need—to articulate the experiences I had lived through. To give back, in a way that felt genuine to me. I've been fortunate to witness a myriad of experiences, to create extensively, and to observe the music business from multiple perspectives. At a certain point, the only course of action that resonated with me was to share my wisdom. Not from a pedestal, but through the lens of my real-life encounters.

Drawing from days and nights of doubt, lessons from failures, and defining moments that shaped who I am today.

The title *Bait to Plate* came to me in silence—not from a brainstorming session, but from prayer. I was still. I was asking for direction. And then it came. Like a whisper from a spiritual ancestor. It landed so clear I could feel it in my chest. I knew this was the name.

This was the process. The late nights were endless marathons spent in cramped,

windowless, stifling studios, where the air was a dense fog of stale smoke and unrelenting ambition. Countless hours spent obsessively perfecting tracks, meticulously tweaking beats, pouring my heart and soul into every note. Everything I had endured—from the insulting 5-year term contracts thrown my way with no advance to help keep me afloat during college, where I held onto my dreams with a grip so tight— to the triumphant moment I clutched my first publishing check, a gleaming six figures, the paper crisp and the ink vividly fresh.

Every experience testified to my struggle and victory, each challenge adding a new layer to the sculpture of my career.

It's like casting a line with purpose, carefully crafting the bait with foresight. You release it into the vast waters of the world, trusting that eventually, a catch will happen. Not immediately, and rarely as anticipated, but with patience and true alignment, it will arrive.

What I've realized over time is this: you can't expect to catch a deep-sea bass casting your line in a shallow lake full of minnows. A lot of folks are standing at the edge of familiar waters, repeating the same moves, the same methods, with the same bait they were taught early on—then wondering why nothing bites, or why the catch ain't feeding the way it used to.

But truth is, if you want a different kind of outcome, you should cast in a different direction. You must study the waters. Learn the shifts. Switch your bait. Switch your location. Sometimes even switch your hands and posture. That's how this game works too. You can't fish for something big in a pool that was never designed to hold it.

And when I say that, I'm not just talking about music. I'm talking about mentality. Business. Intention. Placement. Strategy. Timing. Energy. Alignment. You've got to be real with yourself about where you are and what you're fishing for—then be willing to move, adjust, and evolve for the results you want.

You just need to know how to bait, how to cast, how to wait, and when to reel in. That's what this book is. A guide. A blueprint. A lived map. Because I know what it's like to stand in cold water, casting all day with nothing biting—and I know what it feels like to finally catch something that feeds generations.

What I see when I scroll? I see confusion. I see frustration. I see seasoned artists—artists with plaques and tours under their belt—suddenly feeling lost in an industry that feels nothing like the one they came up in. I see independent creators putting out brilliant work, but unsure of how to move, how to cut through. And I see people stepping away altogether—walking away from music, not because the passion left, but because the system feels too unfamiliar to navigate.

INTRODUCTION

But let me tell you something.

The system isn't broken. It's different. And if it's different, then we need to be different too. That's why I wrote this. Not to tell you how to go viral. Not to force you back into an industry that drained you. But to give you perspective, to offer you tools, to help you build a mindset that adapts. That pivots. That sees change not as a death sentence but as a new chapter.

The music business isn't gone. It's just morphed. It's digital now. It's algorithmic. It's content-heavy. But under all of that, it's still about creation. About connection. About people. You just need sharpened eyes to see the blueprint, refined ears to hear the rhythm of this next wave.

If you're reading this, it means the passion's brewing, or still there. Even if it's flickering, it's alive. And that matters. That passion, when paired with strategy and faith, becomes a power source. It becomes leverage. It becomes legacy. The kind of legacy that creates generational change, not just Spotify numbers. The kind of legacy that feeds your future.

This book is filled with real tools—practical ones. Ways to navigate, to adapt, to create even when the conditions shift. Because they will shift. But like any good fisherman, your job isn't to control the water. Your job is to prepare, to watch, to cast when the time is right—and to keep your hands steady when the catch pulls back.

Even in fishing, some of the best meals come from the hardest fish to catch. You don't always catch it on the first cast. Or the tenth. But if you refine your bait—your skillset, your offer, your creativity—and if you understand where to fish, who to fish with, and how to nourish what you reel in, you can create something powerful.

This book isn't just about the catch. It's about the process. The patience. The pivot. It's about the unseen part of the journey—the early mornings, the doubt, the silence, the rerouting. It's about how to prepare in such a way that when the opportunity does hit, you're not scrambling. You're ready. You're aligned. You're built for it.

So, let's get to it.

Let's sharpen the hook. Let's fix the line. Let's bait it with purpose. Let's make the plate worth it.

It's time to fish like your future depends on it. Because it does.

As you read, ask yourself: what is your bait? Where are you casting it? And are you preparing for the plate, or still just watching the water?

That's when your creativity becomes currency. That's when your talent becomes provision—not just for yourself, but for your team, your family, your future.

But catching the fish isn't the end—it's just the beginning. Just like a fisherman prepares the catch for the plate, you must prepare your gift for the world. You refine the mix. You structure the business. You protect your rights. You clean up the record, package the brand, label it properly—and only then do you serve it to the masses.

And if you cast with intention—if you put yourself in the right rooms, on the right platforms, with the right energy—you'll attract the big fish: the exec who gets it, the agent who fights for you, the producer who respects your craft, the sync director who hears your vision, the DJ who plays your song to thousands, the algorithm that turns your post into a viral movement.

In this world, your gift is your bait. Your voice. Your beat. Your instinct. That spark you carry is the very thing you cast into the ocean of the entertainment industry—hoping, planning, and believing it will catch something real.

Bait to Plate isn't just a metaphor—it's the model. It's how I built a career from scratch, using what I had, refining what I learned, and casting my creativity into the right waters.

1

The Roots of Your Creative Foundation

"Before there was a placement... before there was a publishing deal... there was the basement."

It all starts with appreciation. And truthfully, most of us forget that. We say we're self-made —that we did this all on our own because we put the hours in. My first mixtape I recorded as a fifteen year old artist was called, "Self Made". But that's only part of the truth. Because even the hours you put in were made possible by something or someone that came before. A space. A roof. A hand. A hallway conversation that shifted your mindset. Or a parent who gave you just enough to keep you dreaming.

For me, it began in my mother's basement. That was my first studio. Not because it had the best sound or gear, it didn't. But because it gave me space. Space to create. Space to imagine. Space to shape myself before I ever shaped sound.

Music, film, entertainment, it's all rooted in creativity. But creativity without structure is chaos. What I learned early on is that success is born at the intersection of creativity and structure. Spirit and discipline. Divine inspiration and human execution.

And before any of that, it starts with the mind. The mindset. Because in this game, you can be talented, you can be creative, you can even be well-connected—but if your mindset isn't rooted in something real, you won't last.

Here's the first truth: you can't do this alone. I know you want to. I know you think you have to. But the real power comes when you drop that myth and recognize what collaboration really is. It's not just "doing music" and hoping to get rich. That's the lottery approach. It's aligning with intention. It's understanding that value is created when we recognize value—in ourselves and in others.

The drums are just as valuable as the lead vocal. The guitar loop, the harmonies, the silence in a beat—they all matter. Just like every person you'll meet in this journey. From the aerospace lady I sat next to on a flight, to the record label intern who later became a music supervisor. Every handshake—even the ones that didn't turn into a deal—shaped me.

That's why I can share this now. Because I've lived this. I've been in the rooms—from the basement sessions to the boardrooms. From SoundCloud leaks to Disney placements. It's not just about talent. It's about recognizing the layers—the full system—that surrounds creativity.

This is what I call going from bait to plate. You attract, you learn, you shape-shift... but you never forget the roots.

* * *

Reflect: Who are your creative ancestors? What overlooked moment or space gave you your first real push? Don't skip over that part. That's your foundation. And if your foundation is strong, the rest can be built to last.

2

Discover Your Value

"If you don't value your own art, you'll end up negotiating from hunger—not from worth."

Music found me in my household. It was never a decision—it was an inheritance. My father wasn't classically trained, but he didn't need to be. He played guitar, sang, and wrote songs with an instinctive understanding. He taught himself melody, instruments, and even notation, guided purely by feel and ear. That frequency was always around me. Growing up I watched as my Dad actively pursued his musical gift. He'd constantly work on his craft and devote time to rehearsals with his gospel group, "The Young Prophets". The music became part of me. It created a vibration that moved my soul before I even knew what music business meant.

But I had to find the value in it. I had to recognize that this wasn't just a hobby— it was a lifeline. The same way people value jobs, degrees, certifications… I had to see my gift with that level of seriousness. Because if you don't value what you create, the world will offer you the lowest bid. And worse—you'll take it.

Value is what shapes how you move. When I valued my ideas, I stopped giving them away. When I valued my time, I stopped pulling up to sessions for the vibe. I showed up to make records. To build legacy. To offer something real that could live beyond me.

And value doesn't come from charts. Or applause. It comes from knowing what your roots are, what inspired you, and why this means more than money. Michael Jackson. Bob Marley. Missy Elliott. Kirk Franklin. Big L. Nas. These weren't just artists—they were architects of identity. I valued them because they moved me. That's how I knew music was powerful.

I studied lyrics. Wrote love letters. Filled countless composition notebooks with bars before I had a mic. I knew this mattered. It was personal. And eventually, it became spiritual.

When you treat your music like it matters—when you document it, protect it, refine it—the industry starts to reflect that same value back to you. Not overnight, not all at once. But piece by piece, the world gives you what you believe you deserve.

That's why I'm here—sharing what I know. Because I learned that the music business doesn't start with a contract. It starts with self-worth. It starts with knowing your music is worth protecting, worth negotiating, worth building around.

Your creativity is an asset. Your catalog is equity. Your story is currency. Don't undersell it.

* * *

Reflect: What inspired your journey into music? What part of your creativity do you overlook, or give away too easily? Start valuing it— not just emotionally, but structurally, spiritually, and financially.

3

Studio Essentials, Workflow & Tools

"The creator needs space. You need a space to create. Find your space and make space."

Early on, I learned that the space I was creating in was just as important as the sound I was making. Curating your creative environment goes beyond equipment —it's about finding a space where your mind can isolate melodies, ideas, and concepts that flow freely throughout a session. For me, even the ambiance—the atmosphere and aura of a room—plays a vital a role. Something as simple as the lighting can shift the mood entirely and set the tone for how you create. Whether it's dim, or bright, warm or cool, it all depends on your preference, but being intentional about it matters. The right energy invites the right ideas. And just as important is the space to store and present the work you create and record. If you don't prepare for that, you risk hitting walls in your workflow. When the space supports the process, the workflow becomes instinctive. I remember seeing all the old heads keep stacks of floppy disks, cassettes, and vinyls—that was how you stored music back then. That was their external drive. As you continue to produce demos, ideas, and full song concepts, you'll need a reliable system to store and present your work. There will always come a point when you exceed the limit of your devices' storage. Whether it's your computer, hard drive, or even your cloud space.

This is where many producers experience a sudden halt in their workflow, not because of a lack of creativity, but because of overlooked infrastructure. The more files, plugins, sample libraries, and components you add to your setup, the more critical it becomes to manage your storage and system performance. Keeping this in mind early will protect your momentum and ensure your production flow stays uninterrupted. As a creator, you need to be able to store what you make, revisit it, and grow from it.

When I first got into recording, I didn't have access to a studio. I made a studio. I used my closet, connected an XLR mic to my audio interface, routed it into my computer, and learned how to turn the gain just right so my vocals didn't clip. I figured out how to see the signal coming through. If that line stayed flat I knew something was wrong. That's how I learned routing. That's how I learned levels.

Everything was self-taught. I spent hours just trying to get my voice to record. Just trying to hear playback. Trying to figure out why my session sounded thin, and muddy. I learned that if you want to work in this business, you need to be technical. You can't just only vibe. You have to know how to navigate and adapt your system.

My first real studio session, with professional audio quality and equipment, came from winning a contest. The prize was a full studio recording session with an engineer, and that experience changed everything for me. It was the first time I truly heard what professional sound quality was supposed to be. I'll never forget hearing my own voice back through those speakers—it sounded so clean, so crisp —nothing like the recordings I made in my makeshift setup at home. I asked the engineer, Stanley, how he made the vocals sound that clean. He broke it down: compression, limiters, dynamics. At the time, those were like gibberish to me, but from that moment, I was determined to figure it out. I was hooked. The mission became clear: learn the tools, study the process, and chase that level of sound on my own. Because no matter what, the goal was always quality.

STUDIO ESSENTIALS, WORKFLOW & TOOLS

I was using Sony Acid Music Studio. I learned how to install software. How to build a session from scratch. How to add loops. How to record vocals. How to structure a beat. I was also playing, "Music Maker", and "MTV Music Generator" music making video games on PlayStation—it helped me learn arrangement, just using button commands and interacting with the sequencer. That's how deep I was in the process of figuring it out.

It's a lot of math and science EQ, frequencies, LUFS, reverb decay—it all connects. I realized school wasn't irrelevant like I thought. I'll never forget the major gem while creating music in the Cayman Islands with my friend, JG. He taught me that to get your reverb timing just right, specifically the pre-delay and decay—you can use a simple formula: take 60,000, divide it by your BPM, then divide that by multiples of four. That gives you the precise timing for syncing reverb to your vocals and instruments. When I first learned this, I was mind—blown. Most people have no idea this even exists. I'm grateful JG shared that formula with me. It showed me how much the roots, the math, the science, and the fundamentals all contribute to the more advanced layers of music. Honestly, there's so much depth to this, I could write an entire book on the science of frequency and sound design. But I'll stay on task for now. A lot of the formulas and logic actually applied to how I was learning to make music. I didn't need the most expensive gear. I needed consistency. I needed space. And I needed to optimize my workflow.

I used to create CDs using a 7-to-1 burner, made artwork in Photoshop, and packaged everything by hand. My studio was my bedroom. My desk was my workstation. And I treated it with the same focus a major studio would.

Eventually, I started building a system. I exported all my files in proper folders. I labeled sessions. I had multiple external hard drives for stems, beats, vocals, samples, and more. I made room for my ideas. That's what allowed me to build—because when it's time to send a record, you need to have it ready. Not scattered.

That's what I mean when I say workflow is survival. If you're trying to run a business off your creativity, your creativity has to be organized. That's what separates the hobbyist from the professional. In no time—and with consistency, admiration, dedication, and organization—you'll find yourself steps closer to elevating your gift into a career. A path that leads to recognition, placements, accomplishments, and the kind of success that reflects the work you've been putting in from day one.

* * *

Reflect: Are you creating a system around your creativity? Do you have space for your ideas to grow—physically and digitally? What can you organize right now to improve your workflow and protect your momentum?

4

Building Skills from Scratch

"I had a basement, a cheap mic, a hand-me-down PC and that was enough to start."

Before the placements, before the contracts, before anyone even knew my name... I was just a kid with a cracked version of Logic Studio, some blank CDs, and a belief that I could figure it out.

I didn't have the best microphone. I didn't have a professional soundproof booth. My "studio" was a closet with blankets tacked up to the wall. I had an interface I barely understood, but I learned how to connect my mic with an XLR cable, adjust gain, test input channels—all from scratch. No YouTube tutorials. No manuals. Just error, trial, frustration, and showing up again.

My PC wasn't a powerhouse. But it had a hard drive, and that meant I had space. And space is all a creator needs. I didn't wait to get in a professional studio. I built one. I set up the sessions. I created sounds, dragged loops into timelines. I used the metronome, matching the tempo of my beat box rhythm. I pressed record. I learned how to hear myself. I learned how to correct myself.

I had to teach myself everything—from how to install software, to how to bounce a track. I had to learn why latency mattered. I had to figure out what BPM felt right for my flow. I had to learn EQ and reverb because my mixes were trash and I wanted them to sound better.

I spent countless hours just trying things. Moving through menus. Twisting knobs. Testing settings. Not even making songs sometimes—just learning how to record properly. Learning how to mix without clipping. Learning why I needed to turn down the preamp. Why mono vs. stereo mattered. Why every plugin wasn't a solution—sometimes it was just noise.

I didn't have a mentor. I didn't have a team. But I had a hunger. A real one. I'd record vocals in the closet, come back and listen and be embarrassed by how off it was, but I wouldn't quit. I'd do it again, and again. Until I felt confident with the takes.

The closet became a booth. The booth became a classroom. That computer? That became my studio. My lab. My altar.

And even though the sounds weren't perfect, I was showing up. I was stacking beats. Penning verses. Burning mixtapes. Creating cover artwork in Photoshop. Burning 7 CDs at a time on a duplicator and selling them hand-to-hand. That's how I learned structure—through doing.

I remember figuring out how to route channel 1 and 2 for the interface input—and feeling like I just cracked the code. And I had. Because when you're self-taught, every "aha" moment is a reward. It reassures your growth, and ownership.

There were no shortcuts. There was no cosign. Just raw time and passion.

I had to teach myself how to create space. Not just on my hard drive, but in real time. In my environment. That meant backing up sessions, saving ideas, labeling files properly. Because if I didn't treat my work with care—who would?

This is what most people don't see. They see the placements. They hear the clean mix. But they don't see the kid trying to figure out how to make vocals even record.

That's where the real skill is built. When no one's watching. When there's no reward except getting better.

If you're just starting, don't wait for the studio. Create the space. If you've got a mic and a laptop, you've got enough to build with. Just start. Keep stacking. Keep learning. Keep repeating. As we like to say, "stay cookin'."

Eventually, that rough mix will turn into a solid record. That closet, or basement session will turn into a placement. That curiosity will turn into a career. It happened for me.

***

> Reflect: What's stopping you from learning what you need to learn? What can you build with what you already have? Perfection isn't the starting point—showing up is.

5

Learning the Business & Protecting Your Music

The Only L's you take is for lessons. "The best way to learn business is to read every contract they put in front of you—twice."

I didn't fully understand the concept of publishing until years into my career. Back then, I thought I had it figured out. I transferred from Clark Atlanta University to Georgia State with one goal—to get into their music production and engineering program. I made that move with purpose. But once I transferred my credits, I was blindsided. No one told me that the program wasn't available to me. It was a heavy disappointment—one that could've easily thrown me off course. Still, I refused to let it stop me. I enrolled in a music education course at Georgia State that gave me just enough insight into publishing to plant a seed. It wasn't everything, but it was something. And that small piece of knowledge became part of the foundation I would build on. Because the truth is, publishing isn't something you fully learn in a classroom anyway, it's something you learn in motion. Through real experience. By managing your catalog, calculating writer shares, navigating contracts, and learning the business one record at a time.

Nobody gave me a crash course on publishing. My school became the emails I got CC'd on. It was the side agreements I had to read at 3 AM before hitting 'send.' It was the meetings I sat through with attorneys, accountants, and A&Rs just listening. Trying to peep game. Trying to understand what I was signing before I signed away my rights.

I didn't understand splits at first. Some sheets would say 100%, some 50%, some 200% I thought something was wrong. But then I learned: there's 100% for the master and 100% for the composition. That's how you get 200%. One side is the sound recording. The other is the actual song.

If you don't know that, you might be giving away more than you realize. And in this industry, the second you get your first placement or your first viral record, people will want a piece. If your business ain't right, that check you thought was yours gets split up, or lost in the sauce fast. Low key, there's something called a black box—a collection of unclaimed royalties, publishing, writer's shares, and more. These funds are often generated through streams, radio play, public performances, and more. However, if your work isn't properly registered or your metadata is incomplete, those royalties go unmatched. Furthermore, if those earnings go unclaimed, they don't just disappear—they sit in a pool that can eventually be collected by someone else. And that someone might not be the rightful author of your music. It might not be you.

I'm grateful I learned this when I did, because most artists don't even know the black box exists. It's just one of many reminders that in this game, the business side is just as critical as the creative. Protect your work, register your songs, and stay on top of your catalog, because nobody will fight for your share like you will.

The PRO your Performance Rights Organization, was my first step into business. For me, it was SESAC. I registered in Atlanta around 2013 when I started writing for real. Once I got songs placed, I knew I needed to register them, or I wouldn't see anything from the spins or performances.

Your PRO is what collects your performance royalties. Radio spins, streaming, TV placements—this is how you get paid. You need to have your songs registered, your splits agreed upon, and your metadata in order. If not, the money either goes unclaimed or goes to the wrong person.

And I didn't always have a publisher. At first, I had to do it myself. I was reading emails, deciphering terms, looking up language I didn't understand. But the more I did it, the more fluent I got. That's what makes the difference between surviving and scaling.

My first TV/film synch came in 2010 with two songs: "Play It Cool" and "Socialite". Both were considered and used in the hit TV show The Game—which, at the time, was my favorite show. I was hype! It felt like everything I had worked for was finally aligning. But the truth is... I didn't do the business right. Not because I didn't care—but because I didn't know. I hadn't yet learned how to register my work properly, how to protect my share, how to make sure I got what was mine. I just knew since the opportunity presented itself, I was taking it!

That moment taught me one of the hardest lessons in music: talent gets you in the room, but understanding the business keeps you in the game (pun intended). Even though I produced and co-wrote both songs, I didn't receive a dime from those placements for years. I remember hearing from my collaborators—they got small checks, they were paid. Meanwhile, I was just happy the song was out there, knowing deep down I hadn't handled the paperwork. That was on me. It hurt—but it taught me.

This is a prime example of how experience, real-life trial and error, is where the most important lessons come from. I don't regret it. It made me sharper. Hungrier. Wiser. And if you're reading this, let my early misstep be your early warning: do the paperwork, handle your business, and never let your gift go unclaimed.

When I think about developing a business mindset, I always go back to my moms. She made it a point to push me, no matter how excited I was about the music, to slow down and read the contracts.

She would always say, "Don't just sign—read what you're signing." That was my mother's go-to. A line she repeated more times than I can count. Looking back, I know she probably thought it was going in one ear and out the other. And to be fair, at the time, it kind of was. I was focused on the music. I was young, locked in on the dream, and just wanted to create. Paperwork wasn't exciting to me—it felt like it got in the way. But the older I got, and the deeper I got into the industry, her words started showing up in real time.

Then there was another saying that always stuck with me too:

"Don't count all your eggs before they hatch."

That one came from my great-grandmother. She had this quiet wisdom about her—sharp, practical, and grounded. She was a strong financial steward, someone who had a natural sense for business, saving, and accounting long before any of us even thought about the music business. Her words were legacy, passed down with weight, with intention. And as much as I didn't always show it, they stuck with me.

My mom carried those lessons forward. She loved me deeply, supported everything I wanted to do—but she was cautious. Because she knew the shark-eat-shark nature of the music business. She'd seen it twist people, burn them out, chew them up and spit them out. Especially young Black artists. She feared I'd get caught up in the lights, the passion, the dream—and overlook the paperwork. The ownership.

She had this deep-rooted sense of protection, and it came from generational wisdom. She used to reference an old saying:

"If you want to hide something from a Black person, put it in a book."
—Malcolm X.

As harsh as it sounds, that quote stuck with her. It didn't come from judgment—it came from truth. It was a reflection of how systems were built to keep knowledge gated. To make sure we were talented, but not informed. Seen, but not secure. Valuable, but not empowered.

That's why she was so adamant about education. About being sharp. She didn't want me to just sign things and hope for the best—she wanted me to know what every signature meant. To never be in a room where someone else understood my worth more than I did.

Her prime example? The infamous story of New Edition.

Coming from Boston, we held Bobby Brown and New Edition in legendary status. To this day, they're still one of the greatest R&B groups to ever do it. But the story of their early deal always rung through the streets. After everything—the hits, the tours, the success— they signed a deal and got $500 and a VCR. That's what they walked away with. Their royalty rate? Something like $1.68. That stuck with me. It echoed in my head every time I got close to an opportunity. It reminded me that talent alone isn't enough—you have to know your business. You have to be ready.

The first time I was handed a deal with pressure to sign fast, I felt that echo:
"Don't just sign—read what you're signing."
I remember one of the first major deals I ever received was with legendary R&B producer and songwriter Manuel Seal. At the time, we were working as a writing collective, hungry and building momentum. Manuel invited us to his studio, and I'll never forget the setting—luxurious, well-designed, everything intentional. The space alone gave me a glimpse into the future I was chasing. It wasn't just a studio; it was a symbol. A reflection of what life could look like if I kept making the right moves. If I followed the right footsteps. If I reached that level of excellence.
Then came the paperwork.
Manuel offered us a deal, and it moved fast. Everyone in the group was excited. People were signing with a quickness. There was this unspoken pressure—like if you didn't sign right away, you'd miss your shot. And if you've been in this business long enough, you already know:
90% of the deals you'll be offered come with urgency.
There's this firepit-under-your-feet type of energy. If you don't answer

fast, you might get burned—or so it feels.

But something in me hesitated. I sat with the deal. I read through it. I didn't sign right away. I was skeptical. There were clauses and phrases that didn't sit right with me—not because I knew exactly what was wrong, but because I *didn't* know. And that was enough reason to slow down.

I took the time to seek legal advice. And let me tell you, the more you seek clarification, the longer it takes. Edits, revisions, conversations—they all extend the timeline. So if a deal is built around urgency, that time becomes friction. And still—I knew I had to take those steps.

The language in that contract? It was coded. Business Latin. The Aramaic of industry structure. The type of language that's not made for you to understand—it's made for you to assume. To gloss over. To trust someone else to explain.

But I remembered what my mom had drilled into me:

"Don't just sign—read what you're signing."

So I did. Line by line. Word by word. I was confused, yes. But I knew enough to know what I didn't know. And that awareness alone made me pause.

This was my first real experience with receiving an agreement. A real contract, tied to a real opportunity. And the way that deal unfolded taught me a lesson I still carry today: if you're not reading the fine print, someone else is—someone who knows exactly what it means.

So I took those warnings seriously. And if you're serious about turning your passion into a career, you should too. Because the last thing you want is to be legendary—with nothing to show for it.

When you finally do partner with a publisher, make sure it's one that actually works for you. Because a publisher is like a bridge. They connect your songs to opportunity. And if they're not pitching, placing, or registering your work properly—you're better off solo with knowledge than attached and in the dark.

Protecting your music is protecting your future. That means registering your songs with your PRO, registering your copyrights with the U.S. Copyright Office, and organizing your metadata—titles, splits, dates, collaborators—all of it. If your song gets placed in a film or commercial, the metadata needs to match exactly. Otherwise, the payment gets held up or misrouted.

The hard part is, most artists don't learn this until after they've been burned. After they didn't get paid. After they heard their song used and didn't know who signed off on it. That's why I wrote this. Because I've been through that confusion—and I came out the other side educated and empowered.

Read your contracts. If you don't understand the language, ask someone. Seek legal advice. If you don't have a lawyer, study one. Google, or ChatGpt everything. Don't sign out of excitement. Don't sign just because they're giving you a little up-front. Know your worth—and then know the terms that protect that worth.

* * *

> Reflect: Have you registered every song you've released? Are you signed up with SoundExchange? Do you know your splits? Can you track your royalties? If not, that's your next step. Your music is your business. Start treating it like one.

6

Networking With Intention

"Your network is your net worth. And the first investment you make is showing up."

I learned this the real way, not from reading it on a motivational quote, but from walking it out in real life. From pulling up to every open mic, seminar, college lecture, radio contest, poetry night, and panel discussion where somebody—anybody—connected to the industry was speaking.

I didn't always know who was going to be in the room, but I knew I needed to be in the room. Jasmine's Café at Morehouse, the talent shows at Clark Atlanta, the sweepstakes I entered I showed up, and when I didn't have something ready, I sprinted to go get it.

That day with the gospel duo, Mary Mary I'll never forget it. I had the chance to give them my demo CD. I told Mary Mary that I was an artist and producer— that I'd love for them to check out my music. I then realized I left my CDs in the dorm. Ran like hell to go get it. Came back out of breath—they were gone. That taught me everything about preparation and presence. If you're serious about this, you stay ready.

I also learned that it's not always about who's on stage. Sometimes, it's the person sitting right next to you. In those classrooms and lecture halls, people used to tell us: network with the one sitting right next to you. That stuck with me. Some of the best people I've worked with were sitting beside me before we ever got in a studio or a red carpet.

See, it's not just about who you know, it's about how you show up in those spaces where those people gather. It's about the intention behind every handshake. It's about being the person who adds value, who shares, who listens, who follows up.

You don't build a network by just exchanging numbers or DMing beats to everybody you see. You build it by building real relationships. For example, by remembering someone's birthday. Congratulating them when they level up. Sharing their wins. Checking in. Sending the thank-you email after the session. That's the difference.

And when it comes to value, let's talk about that. Because in this industry, people will try to set your value for you. They'll offer you less than what you're worth and hope you don't know the difference. That's why you have to define your value early—and you have to believe in it.

Value doesn't mean you're perfect. It means you know what you bring. It means you show up prepared. It means your catalog is organized, your music is professional, your energy is intentional. Value is when you walk into a room and they know you're not playing.

Your name carries weight. Your face card matters. And that comes from consistency, reputation, and alignment. You want to be in rooms where people recognize your effort before they even hear your sound. That's real power. That's network equity.

NETWORKING WITH INTENTION

* * *

Reflect: Who are you connected with right now that you could build with? What value are you bringing to your network—and are you showing up consistently with intention? Who would you like to connect with, and why? Don't just chase access—build relationships that open doors.

7

Understand The Assignment: Sync, Licensing & Placements

"Placements are more than just luck—they're about leverage, preparation, and relationships that stick."

My first major placement came in 2014 as a co-producer on Tinashe's breakout single, "2 On". The record went on to achieve platinum RIAA certification and reached No. 1 on both the Billboard R&B and Rhythmic charts—a milestone moment that marked the beginning of my professional journey in the industry.

I got my first major placement because I put myself in the right place, but I stayed there because I was prepared. This industry doesn't care how hungry you are if you don't have the music ready, the paperwork tight, and the understanding to back it all up.

Let's start with what a placement really is. A placement is when your song—whether you wrote it, produced it, or performed it—ends up being recorded and released by another artist, used in a TV show, featured in a commercial, or lands on a game soundtrack. That's when the music you made in your bedroom, your closet, your basement—now has a market. A real moment.

UNDERSTAND THE ASSIGNMENT: SYNC, LICENSING & PLACEMENTS

For me, my first big placement came from believing in the power of intention and alignment. I wasn't just making beats and hoping someone would hear them, I was actively moving with purpose. I was reaching out, presenting my work, showing up in conversations and inboxes, being proactive with purpose. I connected with managers who had direct relationships with artists and labels, and that connection turned into access. That access turned into a moment. And that moment—one session, one room, one song—became a domino. The energy was right, the timing aligned, the track hit, and it got placed.

But what most people don't see is how that moment happened.

It wasn't just raw talent. It wasn't luck. It was me being attentive, being present, and knowing how to read the room. Inserting myself into a space where I could be useful. Not just standing around waiting to be asked, but sensing the energy, reading the vibe, and identifying the need. That's how I got my first placement. I saw there was a call for my production—something that needed edge, texture, rhythm, movement—and I stepped in. Respectfully, collaboratively, intentionally.

In this case, it meant picking up the production—crafting the drums, 808s, percussion—the entire rhythmic backbone. I brought in ambiance, atmosphere, subtle chants, snapping drum rolls, little flourishes that gave the track personality. I helped construct the structure, define the transitions, and even knew when to *remove* something—like pulling a snap during a hook to let the vocal breathe. That's what it means to serve the record. To elevate the room.

But you only see those details when you're **present**. When you're not in your ego, but in your purpose. That placement came from me asking:

"How can I make this better?"

And then moving on that answer with intention.

The truth is, getting placements isn't just about talent—it's about **hustle and strategy**. There are multiple ways in: through the artist, through their manager, the A&R, the publisher, the engineer, even a close affiliate. Every single one of those lanes is valid. There's no one way. But whatever door you try, you better be ready when it opens.

You don't get ready in the room—you arrive ready. Because that one chance to contribute, that one moment to show you *belong*—it doesn't come with a rewind button. And the only reason I made that placement is because I wasn't just looking for opportunity. I was prepared to be of value the second it showed up.

I used to be the spam artist, for real. Inboxing everybody DJs, execs, influencers—telling them I had heat. Some people ignored it. Some actually listened. And once in a while, somebody responded, and that opened up something. But I learned that you can't rely on spam. You have to rely on building the right relationships and showing up with the right presentation.

Your song has to be curated and placed in the right hands. And when it is, that's where the real business starts. You need to have your producer agreements ready, your publishing splits done, your PRO registration locked, and your copyrights filed, because once the placement goes live, the money's moving, and if you're not in position, you're not in the payout.

Syncs are a bit different, but they carry that same blueprint. If you want to get your music into film, TV, games, and ads—you need to tap into the sync world. That means music supervisors, directors, licensing reps. They need music that fits their vision, their scene, their world. So instead of asking, "Does this slap in the club, or for the radio?" ask, "Does this match the emotion of a scene?"

There's a whole science to creating for sync. You have to think in texture, not just tempo. You might need stems, no lyrics, alternate mixes, clean versions, 15—second edits. The people making these decisions aren't always musicians, they're visual curators. They're looking for what fits, not what's hot. That's why intention matters.

There were placements I got just by keeping in touch with someone who believed in me. Not pitching aggressively, just letting them know what I had ready. I've had friends who became sync reps, producers who became music directors, interns who became gatekeepers. You never know who's going to

UNDERSTAND THE ASSIGNMENT: SYNC, LICENSING & PLACEMENTS

open the door later—so treat everyone like they might.

And understand, sometimes a sync deal won't come with a big check upfront. Sometimes you get more value from the exposure than the budget. I've taken smaller fees to build my catalog, to get a co-sign, to establish leverage. And that leverage eventually led to better deals, bigger licensing checks, and partnerships with major entities.

Every record you release, every deal you do, every connection you foster adds to your value in this space. The more songs you have placed, the more your publishing is worth. And when you've got real catalog value, you can go beyond placements—you can start talking acquisition.

* * *

Reflect: Do you have songs in your vault that fit a scene, a film, a world beyond just radio? Are your split sheets, registrations, and rights secure if that opportunity knocks? It's not just about making music—it's about preparing it for the plate.

8

Leverage is The Long Term Play

"This game is a team sport—but you better know how to run your own plays."

After my first big placement, everything changed. The phone started ringing more. The emails hit faster. People I hadn't spoken to in years suddenly wanted to connect again. And I realized real quick—success brings company, but it doesn't always bring clarity.

Everyone wants to be on your team when you're winning. But if you don't know how to lead your own business, you'll end up in a team that's exhausting you instead of maximizing for you.

The music business is built on teams—managers, lawyers, publishers, agents, CPAs. At some point, you'll need these roles. But the real key is understanding what they do before you bring them in. Because if you don't know what you need, you'll hire based on pressure or hype—and that's a trap.

When I signed my publishing deal, I had two managers, an attorney, and a CPA. Sounds like a full squad, right? But each of them took a percentage. So when that first real check hit, I watched it get split up before I even touched it. Between 30% for management, 5% for the attorney, 5% for accounting, and more—that check thinned out fast.

I realized then that every person you bring on board eats off your plate. So you better know what each one is bringing to the table. Is your lawyer reading your deals or just passing them along? Is your manager creating opportunities or just reacting to the ones you bring? Are they pushing you or just cashing in on you?

Ownership became the word that mattered most to me. Because once I started understanding that every song I made was IP intellectual property I started moving different. Every beat, every vocal, every file, every split sheet… it all meant something. It all had future value.

If you don't control your masters, if you don't know your splits, if your contracts are vague, you are building someone else's legacy with your name on it. And I wasn't about to let that happen.

So I got structured. I created folders on my computer for every piece of business. Contracts, split sheets, invoices, vendors, royalty statements. I tracked who did what. I tracked when it was submitted. I started thinking like a business, not just an artist. Because art without ownership is bondage. It's a Queen with no throne.

And even with a team, I stayed involved. I read every agreement. I asked every question. I wanted to know the breakdown of every deal, not just the advance, but the recoupment, the backend, retention period, the term length, the sunset clause. Because when it's your name on the paperwork, you have to live with what's inside.

Your team should empower your ownership—not extract it. And every deal you sign should make your catalog stronger, your reach bigger, your vision clearer. If it doesn't, it's not the right deal. No matter how good the check looks.

*　*　*

Reflect: Are you running your business—or is your business running you? Do you know who's on your team and what they're earning from your work? It's time to take control. Ownership is not just about the masters—it's about your mindset.

9

Shapeshifting Into Ownership

"Independence doesn't mean you're alone—it means you've learned to bet on yourself."

There's a moment in every creative's life where you realize—if I don't steer this ship, it's going to drift.

I had to make a choice, one that most artists don't want to face. As a producer, a performer, a writer, and DJ, I was doing it all—but for too long, I had someone else navigating the wheel. I had a manager. At first, it helped. There's comfort in handing off the phone calls, the contracts, the back-and-forth. But eventually, comfort turned into complacency. And I realized: no one was going to run my business better than me. Not because they didn't care—but because they couldn't possibly care as much as I did.

So I removed the role. The manager went. I stepped into the role myself. Full-time. All in.

I became the president of my own publishing company and production company—not just by title, but by practice. I started managing my catalog, my relationships, my bookings, my sync opportunities, my PRO affiliations, my legal conversations, and even the sessions that needed to be scheduled and closed.

Every decision became mine. Every win, mine. Every loss, mine too.

But through this, I learned how to read deals, how to speak the Aramaic language of contracts. I no longer depended on someone else to tell me what I was worth. I studied the terms. I studied the numbers. I studied the people.

And if I did bring in support—an attorney, a creative partner, a licensing vendor—I made sure I learned from them. That was the difference. I stopped hiring people to carry the load, and instead began building a circle I could grow with. That mindset shift was everything. You don't grow a business by outsourcing all your power. You grow it by learning how to wield it.

Sometimes I had to shapeshift. One season I'm the executive, the next I'm the talent. One day I'm negotiating terms, the next I'm in the studio finalizing post production of a song. But every version of me had the same goal: ownership.

When you manage yourself, you don't just learn how to survive—you learn how to build your own. And once you understand the value of ownership, it's hard to go back to dependency.

At a certain point in this journey, you realize the real win isn't just in getting on, it's in staying on. That's where innovation becomes your survival, and independence becomes your greatest leverage.

There's a myth out here that says you need a label to make it.

That without a co-sign, you're invisible.

That unless someone from the inside pulls you up, you're just like a crab in the barrel—climbing, trying to make it out, but constantly overlooked. Unheard. Unvalidated. Like you don't matter until someone already championed in the industry says you do.

And for a long time, I believed that myth.

I used to sit, imagining what a co-sign from somebody like Timbaland, or Pharrell would've done for me. As an up-and-coming producer, artist, songwriter—I imagined how different the path might look. It wasn't even about being starstruck. It was about what that level of validation unlocked. The access. The rooms. The energy. To be able to create in the same spaces they made hits in, around the same execs, artists, and networks who already respected their work and legacy. That kind of vouch—it moves you. It opens doors before you even walk through them. I thought, *That's all I need.* That single hand to lift me out the static. To say, *He's next.* Because when a giant speaks your name, the industry listens different.

I'd study how Lil' Wayne had Birdman. How Kanye had Jay. They didn't just come in—they came through the gate with torches in hand, labels behind them, the streets, A list publicity, radio ready, cameras rolling. BET. MTV. Full rotation. Their voices echoed in homes and hoods, their videos played on loop like prophecy. And I watched from my city, eyes wide open, thinking. *That's the way in.*

I wasn't chasing hype—I was chasing **momentum**. That domino effect. That ripple from one "yes" that splits the silence. I thought a co-sign was the only way to *not* be invisible.

Coming from where I'm from, it felt like the only real way out. Because truthfully, nobody was passing down opportunities. There were no hand outs, or putting you on just because you had talent. And when the city's cold, and the industry's colder, it starts to feel like without that co-sign— you're stuck in that barrel. Climbing, slipping, gripping the walls, while the ones at the top look down but don't reach back. You're down there with your potential, your prayers, your product—and still invisible.

So yeah—I wanted it. I craved it.

That moment where someone already respected opened the door and said, *This one right here—pay attention.*

I learned early: if I wanted to be respected, if I wanted to be seen, I had to *build* that respect. I had to become the one who could vouch for myself.

I had to shift from chasing a co-sign to becoming the source.

From wanting a handout to making a name for myself.

From dreaming about the room to becoming the reason people wanted to be in it.

And that changed everything.

I realized if I had value, if I moved with structure, and played the long game with strategy, I didn't need a label to validate me. I didn't need to beg for the stamp. I could create my own lane, write my own story, and move my own music—and I could still feed my team, feed my family, and feed myself.

I started asking different questions:

What makes people respect you? Not just follow you, but *respect* you.

The answer? Results. Execution. Consistency. Value.

That became the focus: becoming undeniable without a handout. Building leverage. Building catalog. Building story. I stopped dreaming about being discovered and started working to be remembered. I learned that self-validation backed by real value is louder than a borrowed co-sign.

Because let's be honest—what's more powerful than someone co-signing you?

You co-signing yourself.

You showing up with proof. With receipts. With impact.

You not just asking to be let in—but building the door, the house, and the address they now must come find you at.

That shift in mindset gave me power. I stopped seeking permission.

I became the brand. I became the presence. I became the movement.

And now when I walk into the room, I don't need a name drop to stand tall. I am the name.

I didn't wait on a check to innovate. I didn't wait on permission to distribute. I found a way to turn what I had into something that could grow. From building websites, registering my own works, learning metadata and mastering my own files I leaned into what made me independent, not what made me dependent.

Innovation is also spiritual. It's the ability to see what's not there yet—and build it anyway. When I started thinking about NFTs and music, about integrating my catalog with blockchain, about digital ownership and AI tools I wasn't following trends, I was listening to the future.

The industry shapeshifts every year. It doesn't just evolve—it mutates. What was golden yesterday fades into memory today. Coming up in the late '90s, I caught that moment right after the vinyl era had bowed out with grace. Vinyl

SHAPESHIFTING INTO OWNERSHIP

had its weight—its soul—but by the time I stepped in, it was already becoming archive. The sound was shifting, and so was the hustle.

Cassettes were the currency. Tangible. Personal. And flawed. You'd rewind them with a pen, pray the ribbon didn't snap, and sometimes you'd pull that thing out the deck like you were saving its life. Then came CDs. Sleek. Clean. Fragile. You'd burn your mixtape, write the names in Sharpie, hand it off like a personal statement. But all it took was one scratch and the whole thing skipped like a memory you couldn't quite hold onto. Still, it was progress. That disc felt like the future—until it wasn't.

Because soon came the downloads. The compressed files. The iPods. The transition from something you held... to something you clicked. The tactile became invisible. And once the music left your hands, the business followed.

Manufacturing? Gone.

Packaging? Gone.

Distribution? Rewritten.

No more plastic wrap, no more inserts, no more print. Just code. Just bandwidth.

Then came streams, and now music no longer lives on your shelves—it floats in the clouds. In algorithms. And the game? It's moving even faster now. The format of how we create, how we listen, and how we deliver has been flipped inside out. Every innovation cracks open a new layer. Every year, a new model rises while the old one fades. The labels adjust. The middlemen shift. And artists? We adapt—or we disappear.

But through all that change—there's a constant.

Ownership. And positioning.

That's the part that doesn't shape shift. That's the piece you control—if you build right. While the industry runs like a revolving door, the long game is staying planted. Owning what you create. Positioning yourself where no trend can replace your value.

See, as the formats change, new lanes open. New methods. New models. And that's where the real thinkers eat. You don't just play the game—you learn to build inside it. You watch how technology reshapes the stage, and instead of fighting it, you use it to write your own blueprint. Every innovation in music and tech is an invitation to reimagine how you move.

This is the long game.

It's not just making noise—it's designing systems.

It's not chasing a hit—it's owning a catalog.

It's not begging for placement—it's building presence.

And it's not just keeping up—it's positioning yourself to be unmoved no matter how many times the game spins the wheel.

Because while the industry shifts shapes, I sharpen mine.

Because while everyone's out here chasing that quick hit—the viral spike, the algorithm wave—I started realizing the real win was in the long game. Not chasing the firework, but building the foundation. Not just being heard—but being set up. Residuals. Royalties. Passive income.

That's independence.

Not just being unsigned—but being unshaken.

Knowing that no matter how the platforms evolve, no matter what they call the next wave—*you still own the current.*

Your catalog becomes your currency. Your brand becomes your backbone. And your structure? That's your freedom.

This game will flip itself over and reinvent a thousand more times. AI, virtual stages, blockchain, whatever's next—I welcome it. Because I've built a system around legacy. Around *value*. Around the type of control that doesn't expire with a trend.

That's the power I learned to chase.

And once you taste that kind of freedom, you stop looking for the label to sign you...

And you start working like you're the one they gotta catch up to.

But don't get it twisted. Independence doesn't mean isolation. Still collaborate. Still build with others. But do it with intention. I enter every situation with my structure already solid. That way, any partnership enhances my platform, it doesn't define it.

You have to ask yourself: Are you building a business that can survive without someone else's budget? Are you planting seeds that will grow even if the spotlight moves on? That's the real long-term play.

Your IP is your equity. Your catalog is your currency. Your consistency is your campaign. That's the formula.

I've seen too many artists chase short wins. Sell off everything just to post about the check. That's not my wave. I'm here for legacy. I'm here to eat now—and later. That's why I structure every deal to make sense not just in the moment, but for the marathon.

* * *

> Reflect: What are you building that will still feed you five years from now? Are you innovating, or are you imitating? Do you have ownership—or just opportunity? The future belongs to the ones who prepare today.

10

Legacy, Longevity & Feeding the Future

"Legacy ain't about what you leave behind—it's about what keeps feeding others when you're gone."

I remember the first time I tasted *merluza negra*—the Patagonian toothfish. I was deep in Tierra del Fuego, the southernmost tip of Argentina, a place that already felt like a world within itself. That fish? Probably the best I've ever had in my life—buttery, rich, clean. But what made it even more special was learning how it's caught. These aren't fish you just stumble upon. They're found in waters over a thousand meters deep, sometimes even two thousand. You need longlines with thousands of baited hooks, the right conditions, and serious patience. And even then, nothing's guaranteed.

It reminded me of what it really takes to catch something great—not just in the sea, but in music. Catching a hit song, a major placement, or even finding your sound—it's not some quick grab. It's deep work. Like dropping your line into the abyss and waiting... adjusting your bait, switching your strategy, staying locked in.

As a producer, artist, and songwriter, I've had hundreds of sessions. From buzzing newcomers to major-label artists. There are sessions you walk into with all the hope in the world—new energy, new synergy—and still, nothing lands. Many times the song just ends up living as a draft on some hard drive.

That's real. That's the game. Not every hook catches. Just like fishing those Patagonian waters, sometimes it takes more than one drop, more than one day, more than one approach.

But when the conditions are right, when your bait is strong, your technique is refined, and your persistence lines up with preparation, that's when you pull something up from the deep. Something rare. Something special. I've learned that in both life and music, the biggest catches don't come easy. You gotta cast over and over again, refine your tools, adjust your line, learn from every missed bite. You might not even realize you're preparing for the big one until it hits.

And when it hits? That hit song, that life-changing sync, that perfect record—it nourishes. It feeds your future. Like that merluza negra, it's not just a meal, it's a moment. A result of depth, patience, alignment, and craft.

From bait to plate—it's not just a saying. It's a process. It's a mentality. And if you stay with it, stay open, keep refining and casting with intention—you'll bring something rare to the surface.

Everything in this journey led me here. From the basement studio sessions to performing with my idols. From spam DMs to closed-door meetings with labels. From burning CDs in a dorm room to seeing a song I produced on national TV. Every moment, every lesson, every loss, and every win, it all became part of the legacy I'm building. The future favors the prepared—not just the privileged. It belongs to those who are built to last. I had to realize that everything I was doing, every deal I signed, every song I touched, every late night I pushed through—was either feeding a fleeting moment or feeding the future.

There was a shift that happened in me, and I want to share that with you.

I stopped making music just for the now. I started making it with tomorrow in mind. Because truth be told, I've seen songs go from being skipped in a session to being synced in a major film two years later. I've seen melodies that collected dust on hard drives become the heartbeat of viral movements. Music is timeless, but only if you treat it that way.

One of the best examples is the record *"Running Up That Hill"* by Kate Bush—released in 1985, yet reborn decades later through a viral wave on TikTok. A whole new generation heard that record for the first time like it was brand new. That's not luck. That's legacy.

I had to adapt this mindset as both an artist and a music business owner—not just someone participating in the system, but someone designing the system around me. I had to shapeshift because my business model demanded it. The industry moves like waves, and if you don't learn how to swim with the current—or redirect the stream, you'll be pulled under. And trust me, it's easy to drown when you're carrying the weight of artistry and business without direction.

But the key is: direction exists. Structure exists. Innovation exists.

We are in a time now where the old models are breaking, and in their place are tools—digital tools, AI tools, blockchain systems, direct-to-fan access points, creator monetization. You don't have to wait to be discovered anymore. You can design your own discovery.

The tools we have now allow us to re-release music in multiple versions, offer exclusive content directly to our listeners, license music across borders, and collect royalties in real-time. There was a time when that was unthinkable. But now, it's at your fingertips.

Streaming changed the game. At first glance, it can seem like it devalues the work—a fraction of a penny per play? But when you break down the math, as economists like Will Page have shown, streaming can actually outperform the old model if you understand its structure. Instead of being paid once per broadcast (one-to-many), you're being paid per interaction—meaning the more direct, personal engagement you create, the more potential your catalog holds. That's scalable legacy. That's feeding the future.

Innovation isn't just in the tech—it's in how you approach the tech. Are you resisting it because it's new? Or are you embracing it because it expands your reach?

Every season in this business requires you to replant your seeds differently. Some ideas blossom fast, like wildflowers. Others take years to bloom, like oak trees. But both have their place in the garden of longevity. The key is knowing what you're planting—and why.

And even more importantly—who you're feeding.

LEGACY, LONGEVITY & FEEDING THE FUTURE

This book, this message, these lessons... they aren't just for you. They're for the team you'll build. The village that raised you. The family you'll provide for. The artists and creators that will look to you for guidance in five years, ten years—maybe even long after you're gone.

That's what legacy is.

And in the words I've always told myself and now share with you:

"Make sure the plate you serve from feeds more than just yourself."

May your catalog be deep.

May your contracts be fair.

May your vision outlive the moment.

And may your moves today be the reason someone else believes they can make it tomorrow.

Let's feed the future—and build what lasts.

Bait to Plate* is more than a title. It's the philosophy of my entire come-up. The bait? That's your gift. Your voice. Your story. Your originality. The bait is what you cast into the ocean of opportunity—hoping to attract something greater. But the cast? That's your actions. That's showing up. That's being prepared. That's putting yourself in the rooms where it can happen.

In the music industry, the fish are the gatekeepers, the major moments, the life—changing calls. But just casting bait ain't enough. You have to reel it in. You gotta clean it, prepare it, plate it—just like a fisherman brings home dinner to feed the family. That's what I did with every placement, every sync, every deal, every song. I wasn't just trying to 'get on' I was trying to build something that could feed generations.

I think about the contests I entered as a teen—the $5,000 songwriter sweepstakes, winning at the Reggie Lewis center, receiving my first music check while presenting my song, "My People" at a sold out Celtics game. I think about missing the Mary Mary handoff because I wasn't prepared. I think about the closet booth, the Propellerhead Reason studio days, the first mic setup. Those moments weren't losses— they were part of the seasoning. They built the integrity and intention in what I do today.

You learn that it's not about just making music. It's about learning how to manage your workflow, store your sessions, route your inputs, and track your vocals. You learn EQ, compression, LUFS, splits, metadata, publishing rights. Because all of it matters when the world finally hears your sound.

You also learn that the real strength is in relationships—the ones you nurture, not chase. The ones that grow over years, not overnight. The manager who believes in you. The college classmate who becomes an A&R. The DJ who spins your song because you showed up at his party when nobody else did. Relationships are the real distribution network of this game.

Then come the contracts. The splits. The deals. The moments where you decide: Am I gonna sign away this record, or am I gonna build equity with it? You start learning the language of business. You start organizing your folder structure. You start treating every bounce like an asset. Because it is.

Legacy is not one hit. It's a body of work. It's structure. It's having your paperwork in order so your family benefits long after the applause fades. It's teaching your kids what a PRO is, how sync licensing works, what copyright really means. It's owning your masters, your message, your moves.

    I want the kid recording on cracked software to know that the playing field ain't level—but the rules are learnable. I want the artist who feels unseen to know that the slow route is still a route. And I want the producer sitting in a shared apartment right now with a $40 mic to know: that mic can still spark a movement. I'm living proof.

* * *

Reflect: What are you feeding with your creativity? Are you just cooking for likes—or are you feeding generations? Are you capturing your process in a way that others can learn from? Legacy isn't in the song. It's in the system. Make yours strong enough to outlive you.

11

Conclusion

This isn't just about music. This is about provision. This is about legacy. This is about using what you were given—your gift—to feed the future.

By now, you've seen the full journey: from the basement to the boardroom, from raw talent to polished product, from the cast to the catch to the clean cut that feeds a village.

The plate doesn't serve itself. You have to work it. You have to build systems, protect your rights, own your masters, write your splits, read your contracts, and move with intention.

And above all, you have to value your gift. You have to know that what you carry can shift rooms, open doors, and build empires—if you treat it like it matters. You were given this voice, this vision, this talent—not just to shine, but to serve. Use it wisely. Cast it wide. And shape-shift as many times as you need to until your music feeds more than just your ego—until it feeds your family, your community, your legacy.

Now go. Cast your bait. Build your plate. And feed the world.

Epilogue

Thank you. Truly.

For taking the time. For having the patience. For choosing to sit with a book in a time when attention is currency and time is borrowed. My hope is that this isn't just something you read—but something you return to. That these pages serve not as *the* guide, but as *a* guide—one you can walk alongside with your own experience, your own intuition, your own unwavering faith.

Because belief is everything.

Faith is everything.

It gives company to your hope—and what greater company is there?

If this book offered you anything—let it be reminders. The quotes passed down to me by my family. The teachings, the warnings, the love disguised as lessons. I've carried them with me through every deal, every disappointment, every win. And I share them now because I care—not just about this industry, but about you. The reader. The next wave. The one who's about to step into something real.

This book is for the leaders, the creators, the torch-bearers. The ones who will turn stories into sound, vision into value, purpose into power. You're the reason I keep writing, keep learning, keep pouring into what's next. Because I know that when you're done...

you won't just be full.

You'll be able to feed *your* village. Your family. And beyond.

I look forward to sharing more—unlocking more of what's in my head and heart to help lift others up.

More tools. More tips. More truth.

Until then, walk in purpose. Move in wisdom.

And never forget: your plate was made to feed many.

I appreciate you.

- Brendon Allyn Waters

Glossary of Music Industry Terms

A reference guide to key terms used throughout this book.

Advance

An upfront payment from a label, publisher, or platform, typically recouped from future royalties or income.

Advance Payment

A lump sum given at the start of a deal; usually non-refundable and recouped against future earnings.

Admin Deal

A publishing agreement in which the publisher administers rights and royalties but does not own the compositions.

Artist Development

The long-term process of building an artist's brand, sound, image, and commercial value.

Catalog

The full collection of a creator's musical works, including unreleased, past, and published songs.

Clearance

The process of obtaining rights or permission to use a sample, interpolation, or full work.

Copyright

The legal protection granted to the creator of original music or lyrics, ensuring control over how it's used.

DAW (Digital Audio Workstation)

Software used to record, produce, and mix music (e.g., Pro Tools, Logic Pro, Ableton Live).

Exclusive Rights

The legal ability for one party to control the use, distribution, or exploitation of a work—no one else can use it during this term.

First Right of Refusal

A contractual clause that gives a company or partner the opportunity to accept or decline a future offer before the rights can be offered to others.

Independent (Indie)

A music creator or company that operates outside of the major label system.

Intellectual Property (IP)

Any creative content, such as a song, beat, lyric, or idea, that can be legally owned and monetized.

Licensing

Granting permission for music to be used in media like film, TV, commercials, or games, often in exchange for a fee.

Master

The final, polished version of a recording from which all duplicates (streams, CDs, vinyl) are made and monetized.

Mechanical Royalties

Payments made to songwriters or publishers when their songs are reproduced or distributed, whether physically or digitally.

Metadata

The digital information embedded in music files that identifies the track title, artist, contributors, splits, and more—essential for royalty tracking.

Non-Exclusive Rights

A flexible licensing structure where multiple parties can use or license the same work simultaneously.

Performance Royalties

Payments made when a song is played publicly—on the radio, TV, streaming platforms, or live venues. Collected by PROs.

Placement

When a song is licensed or featured in media, or when another artist records and releases your composition.

PRO (Performance Rights Organization)

Organizations like ASCAP, BMI, SESAC (U.S.) or SAMRO (South Africa) that collect and distribute performance royalties.

Publishing
The ownership and monetization of a song's composition—lyrics, melody, and structure—as opposed to the recording.

Publishing Administrator
A company or service that manages registrations, royalty collections, and licensing on behalf of a songwriter or publisher.

Publishing Deal
An agreement where a songwriter assigns publishing rights to a publisher in return for royalty management, creative services, or advances.

Recoupment
The process by which a company deducts prior investments (like advances or marketing expenses) from your future earnings.

Retention
The ongoing ownership or control of rights by the creator or original rights holder, even after a deal ends. Often negotiated in exit terms or reversion clauses.

Royalty Statement
A detailed financial breakdown showing income generated by your music and where it came from.

Sample
A portion of a pre-existing song used in a new recording, often requiring clearance and licensing.

Split Sheet
A document that outlines the ownership percentages of everyone who contributed to a song's writing and production.

Streaming Revenue
Income generated when a song is played on digital platforms like Spotify, Apple Music, or YouTube.

Sync (Synchronization) License
Permission to use music in timed relation with visual media such as film, TV, video games, or advertisements.

Work for Hire

A contractual agreement where the creator relinquishes ownership in exchange for a flat fee, making the hiring party the legal rights holder.

Sources & Resources

The following materials, articles, and references were used to support key concepts, stories, and facts throughout this book. These sources are intended to provide further insight, context, and educational value for readers seeking to explore the business and craft of music more deeply.

Chapter 5 – Publishing & Royalties

TuneCore. (n.d.). What is the black box and what are black box royalties? TuneCore Help Center.

https://support.tunecore.com/hc/en-us/articles/4406899403924-What-is-the-Black-Box-and-what-are-Black-Box-Royalties

Omari MC. (n.d.). Black box royalties explained.

https://www.omarimc.com/black-box-royalties-explained

Chapter 6 – Lessons from the Industry

Rolling Out. (2023, April 18). Bobby Brown reveals humiliating crumbs New Edition was paid.

https://rollingout.com/2025/04/18/bobby-brown-reveals-crumbs-new-edition/

Wikipedia contributors. (n.d.). 2 On. Wikipedia.

https://en.wikipedia.org/wiki/2_On

That Grape Juice. (2024, November). RIAA: 'Nasty' becomes Tinashe's first gold-certified hit since 2014.

https://thatgrapejuice.net/2024/11/riaa-nasty-becomes-tinashes-first-gold-certified-hit-since-2014/

SESAC. (n.d.). About us.

https://www.sesac.com/about/

Easy Song Licensing. (n.d.). We Can —Song copyright holder information.

https://www.easysong.com/search/songs/song-copyright-holder-infor

mation.aspx?s=1904257

Voyage LA. (2018, May 21). Meet Marley Waters of Marley Waters Productions LLC.

https://voyagela.com/interview/meet-marley-waters-marley-waters-productions-llc-hollywood/

Bonus Reflections & Mantras I

"The moment you realize you've been giving away your genius in exchange for validation is the moment you start charging for your value —not your access.

Bonus Reflections & Mantras II

"You are the publisher. The deal. The leverage.
   Stop waiting for someone else to appraise what you were born to build.

Bonus Reflections & Mantras III

"Your creativity is an asset. Your catalog is equity. Your story is currency. Don't undersell it."

Bonus Reflections & Mantras IV

"Ownership became the word that mattered most to me."

Bonus Reflections & Mantras V

> "You don't grow a business by outsourcing all your power. You grow it by learning how to wield it."

Bonus Reflections & Mantras VI

"I stopped seeking permission. I became the brand. I became the presence. I became the movement."

Bonus Reflections & Mantras VII

"If you don't value your own art, you'll end up negotiating from hunger —not from worth."

www.ingramcontent.com/pod-product-compliance
Lightning Source LLC
Chambersburg PA
CBHW030448100526
44580CB00002B/36